JAN 2008

CROSS-SECTIONS
THE M2 BRADLEY
INFANTRY FIGHTING VEHICLE

by Steve Parker
illustrated by Alex Pang

Capstone
press®

Mankato, Minnesota

Edge Books are published by Capstone Press, a Coughlan Publishing Company
151 Good Counsel Drive, P.O. Box 669, Mankato, Minnesota 56002.
www.capstonepress.com

Library of Congress Cataloging-in-Publication Data
Parker, Steve.
      The M2 Bradley infantry fighting vehicle/by Steve Parker; illustrated by
Alex Pang.
      p. cm. —(Edge Books. Cross-Sections)
      Summary: "An in-depth look at the M2 Bradley Infantry Fighting Vehicle, with
detailed cross-section diagrams, action photos, and fascinating facts"—Provided
by publisher.
      Includes bibliographical references and index.
      ISBN-13: 978-1-4296-0092-7 (hardcover)
      ISBN-10: 1-4296-0092-6 (hardcover)
      1. M2 Bradley infantry fighting vehicle—Juvenile literature. I. Title. II. Series.
UG446.5.P348 2007
623.7'475—dc22   2007008078

Designed and produced by

David West 🧍🧍 Children's Books
7 Princeton Court
55 Felsham Road
Putney
London SW15 1AZ

Designer: Gary Jeffrey
Editor: Gail Bushnell

Photo Credits
Sgt. Matthew Acosta 22nd MPAD, 1, 18–19, 21; DoD photo by Chief Petty Officer
Edward Martens, U.S. Navy, 4–5; wikipedia.org, 6–7; SPC5 VINCENT KITTS,
11; SSG BRONCO A SUZUKI; USA, 12; TSGT James Mossman, 14; DoD photo
by Staff Sgt. Shane A. Cuomo, U.S. Air Force, 17; B.A.E Systems, 24; DoD photo
by Staff Sgt. Aaron Allmon, U.S. Air Force, 22; DoD photo by Staff Sgt. Shane A.
Cuomo, U.S. Air Force, 28–29

1 2 3 4 5 6 12 11 10 09 08 07

TABLE OF CONTENTS

THE M2 BRADLEY

For more than 25 years, the M2 Bradley has been at the forefront of U.S. military action around the world. Its main task is to carry troops into battle quickly and safely. The Bradley protects troops, and itself, using strong armor and deadly firepower.

An M2 Bradley crew guards U.S. soldiers in Iraq. The soldiers are advancing toward an enemy weapons site during 2005.

HISTORY OF THE APC

The vehicles that carry soldiers into battle are called Armored Personnel Carriers, or APCs. The Bradley is the latest in a long line of successful American APCs.

EARLY TROOP CARRIERS

APCs are sometimes called "battle taxis." They crisscross the combat zone, moving troops and other personnel to where they are needed most. Until World War II (1939–1945), most soldiers were carried in ordinary trucks. But trucks had no protection against dangers such as gunfire, grenades, and mines.

The German SdKfz 251 was an early half-track APC from World War II. The open top meant the crew was exposed to danger.

HALF-TRACKS

After World War II, many armies began making their own troop carriers. These vehicles had armor for protection and guns for firing back at the enemy. Many were half-tracks. Half-tracks had wheels with tires in front and large caterpillar tracks behind the front wheels.

The U.S. M113 is the world's most widely-used armored fighting vehicle. By 1960, more than 80,000 were made and being used by 40 countries.

DEFENSE AND ATTACK

Gradually APCs were given stronger armor and full-length tracks to ride over the roughest ground. Their guns became more powerful for attack as well as for defense. These troop carriers, such as the Bradley, have become known as IFVs, or Infantry Fighting Vehicles.

The Russian BMP-3 armored fighting vehicle, with its massive cannon, first appeared in 1990.

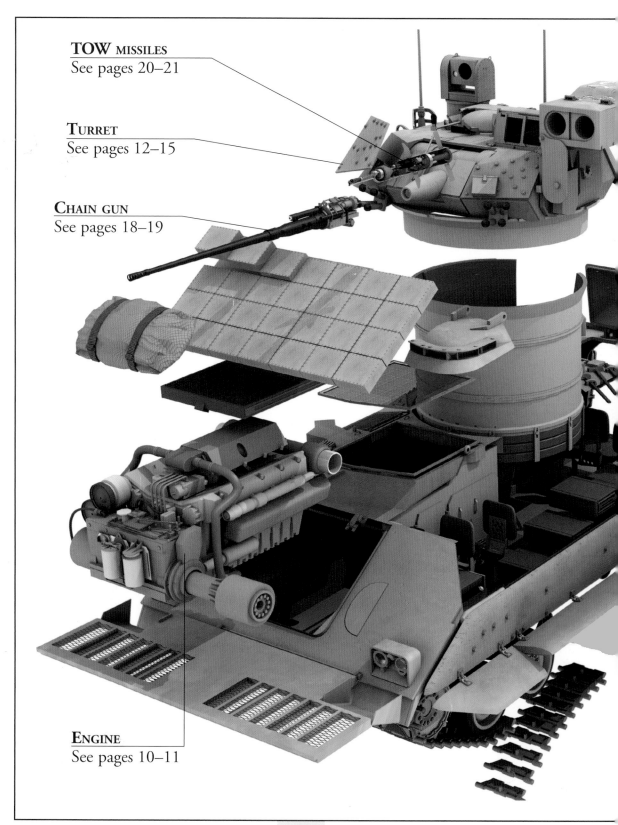

TOW MISSILES
See pages 20–21

TURRET
See pages 12–15

CHAIN GUN
See pages 18–19

ENGINE
See pages 10–11

CROSS-SECTION

The Bradley has a main armored body, or hull. A revolving turret carries the main gun. The engine is in the front, and the troop compartment is inside the rear.

The M2 Bradley is named after General Omar Bradley. He was one of the main U.S. commanders in Europe during World War II. One of the most modern Bradley versions is the M2A3, introduced in 2000.

TROOP COMPARTMENT
See pages 22–23

MANEUVERING
See pages 16–17

M2A3 BRADLEY
Length: 21 feet, 6 inches (6.5 meters)
Width: 11 feet (3.3 meters)
Height: 9 feet, 9 inches (2.9 meters)
Maximum speed (road): 41 miles (66 kilometers) per hour
Combat weight: 72,750 pounds (33,000 kilograms)

ENGINE

The Bradley's speed and acceleration come from its turbocharged diesel engine. The engine is located at the front right side of the hull.

ENGINE SPECIFICATIONS
Cummins VTA-903T
  turbo diesel
Capacity: 903 cubic inches
  (14.8 liters)
Weight: 9,065 pounds
  (4,112 kilograms)

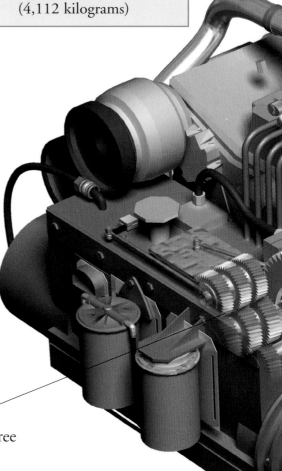

The Cummins engine produces 600 horsepower. The Bradley's fuel tanks hold about 175 gallons (662 liters). With full fuel tanks, the Bradley has a range of about 250 miles (400 kilometers) on roadways.

TRANSMISSION

The HMPT 500-3EC gearbox is automatic, with no gear shift. It has three speed ranges.

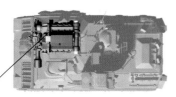

Position of engine on the M2 Bradley

STEERING UNIT

The steering system independently alters the speed of the front drive wheel. A front drive wheel moves the track on either side of the Bradley.

Piston inside cylinder

TURBOCHARGER

The fanlike turbine sucks in extra air and forces it, along with fuel vapor, into the engine. This gives more power. On the battlefield, the engine can run on kerosene-based JP-8. JP-8 is also widely used as a jet fuel.

ENGINE BLOCK

The two rows of four cylinders are set at an angle to each other, giving the name V8. The engine is water-cooled, like a regular car engine. It is also air-cooled by a fan that additionally cools the interior of the vehicle.

The front right hatch opens wide to give mechanics and engineers plenty of space when they work on the engine.

COMMANDER STATION

The commander is in charge of the Bradley. He gives orders to the driver, the gunner, and the soldiers in the troop compartment.

The commander is on the right of the turret, with the gunner to the left. He can stand to look out through the open command hatch on top of the turret. Or he can close this hatch for safety and sit down. When seated, he views the scene through the window and on screens.

Radio antenna

The commander constantly passes information to his crew by using the face-boom microphone and helmet headphones.

COMMANDER'S VIEWER

The Commander's Independent Viewer (CIV), displays sources of infrared, or heat, energy. The viewer gives night vision by sensing "warm" enemy troops, vehicles, and engines in the dark.

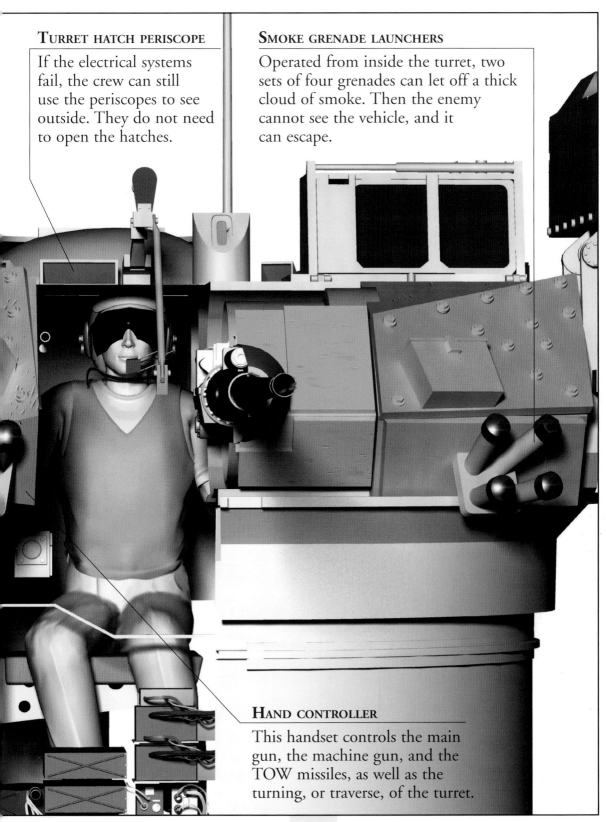

TURRET HATCH PERISCOPE

If the electrical systems
fail, the crew can still
use the periscopes to see
outside. They do not need
to open the hatches.

SMOKE GRENADE LAUNCHERS

Operated from inside the turret, two
sets of four grenades can let off a thick
cloud of smoke. Then the enemy
cannot see the vehicle, and it
can escape.

HAND CONTROLLER

This handset controls the main
gun, the machine gun, and the
TOW missiles, as well as the
turning, or traverse, of the turret.

GUNNER STATION

The gunner sits in the turret, to the left of the commander. He controls the main gun and coaxial machine gun. The commander can take over in an emergency.

The gunner has an array of sensors, sights, and displays to identify possible targets. He checks their direction and distance (range). He controls the firing of the main gun. It can fire single shots with each trigger press or continuously fire up to 200 rounds per minute.

COAXIAL MACHINE GUN

The M240C machine gun is coaxial. This means it points in the same direction as the main gun. It can be fired by either the commander or the gunner.

The gunner and commander (left) discuss which shells may be needed. They are leaving on an escort mission with M1 Abrams tanks and supply trucks.

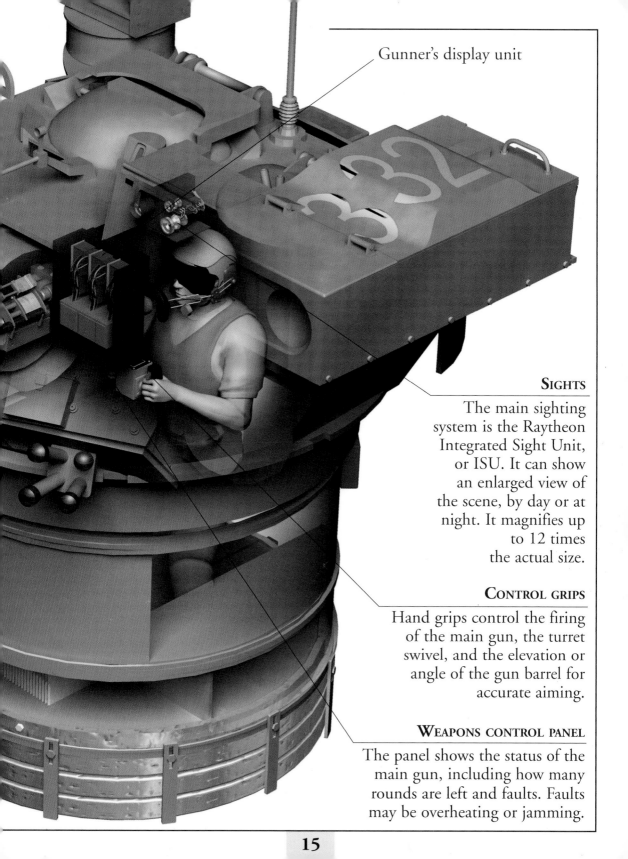

Gunner's display unit

SIGHTS

The main sighting system is the Raytheon Integrated Sight Unit, or ISU. It can show an enlarged view of the scene, by day or at night. It magnifies up to 12 times the actual size.

CONTROL GRIPS

Hand grips control the firing of the main gun, the turret swivel, and the elevation or angle of the gun barrel for accurate aiming.

WEAPONS CONTROL PANEL

The panel shows the status of the main gun, including how many rounds are left and faults. Faults may be overheating or jamming.

MANEUVERING

The third crew member of the M2 Bradley is the driver, who sits in the front left of the hull. He controls the speed, steering, and braking.

The driver can see outside using three forward periscopes and one left-side periscope. In newer Bradleys, there is also an AN/VAS-5 thermal night viewer. The Global Positioning System (GPS) shows the crew's exact position and course.

KEY TO CONTROLS
1. Steering yoke
2. Accelerator pedal
3. Brake pedal
4. Auto transmission lever
5. Speedometer

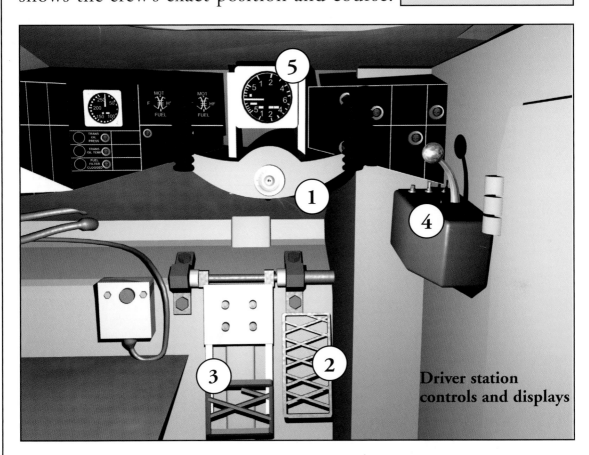

Driver station controls and displays

DRIVER STATION

The driver turns the barlike yoke to steer left or right. He presses foot pedals to speed up or brake. Displays include speed, temperature, and fuel levels.

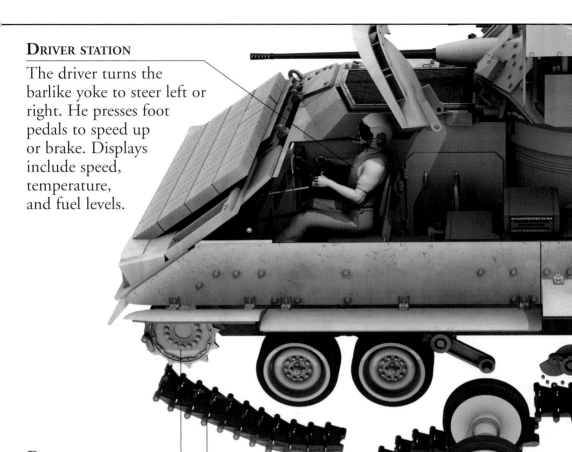

DRIVE WHEEL

The engine turns the drive wheel at the front of the vehicle on each side. The 11 large "teeth" on each drive wheel fit into slots in the track to move the track along.

TRACK

The left track has 84 links, or shoes, and the right track has 82. Each track width is 21 inches (53 centimeters).

ROAD WHEELS

The six road wheels on each side of the vehicle have rubber tires, and turn as the track passes under them. Each wheel has torsion bar suspension with a springy bar allowing the wheel to move. Wheels 1, 2, 3, and 6 have dampers (shock absorbers).

The driver's sight through his vision blocks can be limited by dust.

Chain Gun

The Bradley's main armament is the M242 Bushmaster chain gun. It can hurl deadly shells more than 4 miles (6 kilometers).

A chain gun uses a powered chain loop to load the next round after each firing. (In a recoil gun, the "kickback" force does this.) The M242 Bushmaster fires two main kinds of shells. One is AP, or Armor-Piercing. This shell smashes through armor like a hard metal arrow. The other is HE, or High Explosive, which blows up on impact.

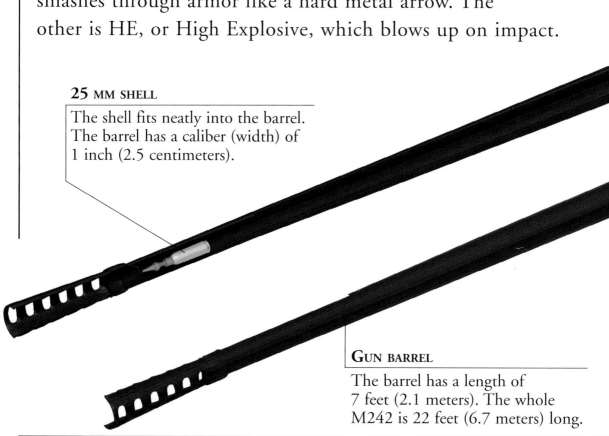

25 MM SHELL
The shell fits neatly into the barrel. The barrel has a caliber (width) of 1 inch (2.5 centimeters).

GUN BARREL
The barrel has a length of 7 feet (2.1 meters). The whole M242 is 22 feet (6.7 meters) long.

The M242 is ready to open fire at any time. In most Bradleys, there are 300 shells loaded and ready. Another 600 can be stowed away for the gunner to load quickly when needed.

LOAD INDICATOR

THERMAL COVER

RECOIL SPRING

TYPES OF SHELLS

AP SHELL
Weight: 1.2 pounds
    (0.5 kilograms)
Range: 6,000 feet
    (1,800 meters)

AP shells fly at 3,900 feet (1,200 meters) per second as they leave the barrel.

HE SHELL
Weight: 1.8 pounds
    (0.8 kilograms)
Range: 10,000 feet
    (3,000 meters)

HE shells fly at 2,641 feet (800 meters) per second as they leave the barrel.

MISSILES

TOW missiles are tracked by sensors on the launcher and shown on the tracking display.

The Bradley's most powerful weapons are its anti-tank TOW missiles. They are fired from the dual launcher on the left side of the turret.

TOW means Tube-launched, Optically tracked, Wire command-link. The missile, enclosed in a tube, is loaded into the launcher. After firing, two long wires extend from the tube and attach back to the launcher. The wires carry signals from the gunner. He watches the display and guides the missile to its target.

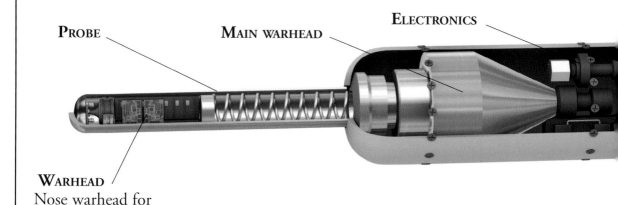

PROBE   MAIN WARHEAD   ELECTRONICS

WARHEAD
Nose warhead for
initial armor puncture

The M6 Bradley Linebacker is a modified Bradley that launches Stinger ground-to-air missiles from four tubes. Stingers are fired at enemy aircraft and missiles.

TOW MISSILE

Early TOW 2 missiles have been improved as TOW 2As and 2Bs. TOW missiles are 4 feet (122 centimeters) long and almost 6 inches (15 centimeters) wide. The TOW missile weighs 50 pounds (22 kilograms). It can be guided to targets up to 2.3 miles (3.7 kilometers) away.

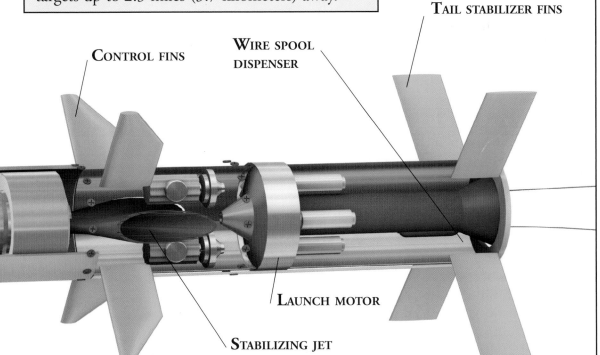

TAIL STABILIZER FINS

WIRE SPOOL DISPENSER

CONTROL FINS

LAUNCH MOTOR

STABILIZING JET

TROOP COMPARTMENT

M2 Bradleys have room in the rear of the hull for six or seven soldiers. The troop compartment also carries all of the soldiers' equipment.

M3 Bradleys look similar on the outside to the M2s, but they are used for scouting and reconnaissance. In their rear compartment are two scout personnel and extra communications equipment, ammunition, and missiles.

ACCESS HATCH AND RAMP

The rear hydraulic ramp lowers to allow troops to enter or leave rapidly. There is also an upper hatch for missile reloading.

In 2006, combat-ready soldiers in Iraq enter an M2 Bradley using the rear ramp.

Rear hydraulic ramp

Upper hatch cover

An infantry member reloads the TOW missile launcher. He uses the upper hatch which gives armored protection.

STORAGE AREAS

Under the bench seats is storage space for equipment and supplies. Equipment varies depending on the mission.

DISPLAY SCREEN

The troop squad's leader can watch the display screen, which shows similar information to the commander's display.

Bradley variants

In addition to the M2 IFV and the M3 CFV, or Cavalry Fighting Vehicle, which is used for scouting, there are other Bradley versions.

The M2A2 ODS-E (Operation Desert Storm-Engineer) Bradley has repair and maintenance equipment. Some Bradleys are used as mobile medical centers. Others have generators for remote electrical power.

The BFIST has the same guns as other Bradleys, plus extra firepower.

BFIST

The M7 is the BFIST, or Bradley Fire Support Team. It has extra computing power and forward observation systems to detect enemies. The M7s provide supporting fire for troops on the ground using guns, grenades, and other armaments.

BRADLEY STINGRAY

The Stingray is a powerful laser mounted on the Bradley's turret. It is designed to detect and disable enemy optical (light-based) sensors. These sensors include binoculars, telescopes, periscopes, gunners' sights, and cameras.

M270 MULTIPLE LAUNCH ROCKET SYSTEM
The Bradley chassis (framework) and tracks are fitted to the M270 missile launcher. The M270 can send rocket-powered, surface-to-surface missiles toward enemy vehicles and buildings.

Bradley chassis and tracks

Tilting twin rocket launcher unit

Total of 12 launch pods

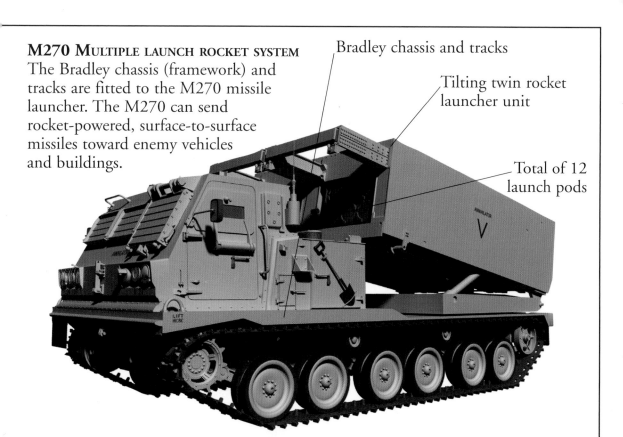

The M270 fires its missiles, then moves before the enemy detects its position.

THE MISSION

M2 Bradleys carry ground troops to conflict areas. They often work with M1 Abrams main battle tanks.

Bradleys and Abrams have similar speed and performance. Bradleys unload infantry troops when an area needs clearing of enemy soldiers. Often these soldiers are hiding among buildings that house civilians. This means that the tanks cannot use their big guns.

5. The Bradley and Abrams commanders wave the all-clear. The crews move on to the next site for clearance.

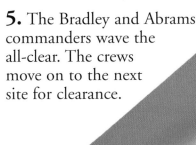

1. An M2 Bradley leading the mission spots a hostile tank on a hill. The tank is guarding the area. The M2's gunner checks the distance and aims. The TOW missile hits.

4. The remaining enemy troops realize that without their APC, they cannot escape. They surrender.

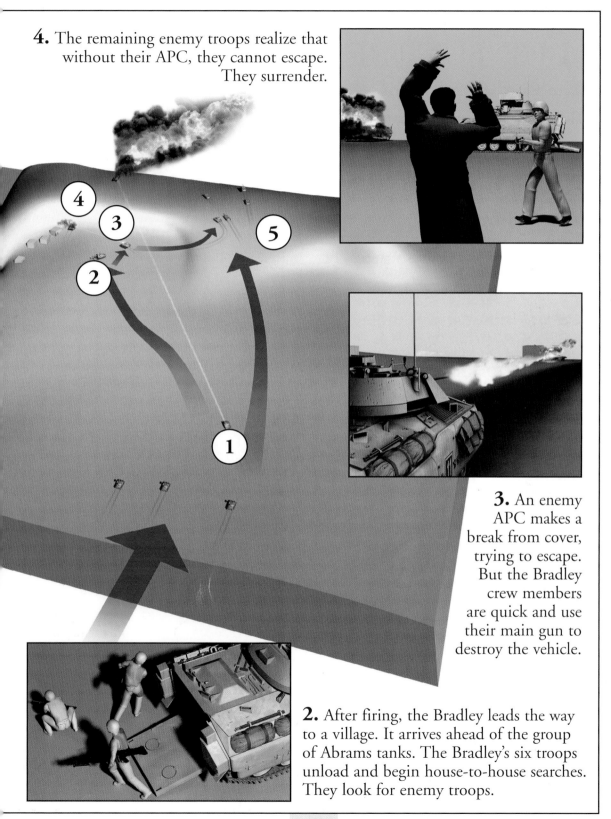

3. An enemy APC makes a break from cover, trying to escape. But the Bradley crew members are quick and use their main gun to destroy the vehicle.

2. After firing, the Bradley leads the way to a village. It arrives ahead of the group of Abrams tanks. The Bradley's six troops unload and begin house-to-house searches. They look for enemy troops.

THE FUTURE

The Bradley family of fighting vehicles is now more than 25 years old. Will it survive for another 25?

Bradleys have proven themselves in many battles, from the Gulf War of 1991 to Operation Iraqi Freedom that began in 2003. Both the M2s and M3s have been improved to M2A3s and M3A3s. These vehicles have better armor, more accurate targeting, and digital communication and electronic systems. The U.S. is developing a new FCS (Future Combat Systems) tank that could eventually replace the Bradley. But the dependable Bradley will be around at least until 2020.

M3A3s head out from a forward base in Iraq in 2004.

GLOSSARY

armor (AR-mur)—a protective metal covering

chassis (CHASS-ee)—the main framework of a vehicle to which the other parts are fixed

horsepower (HORSS-pou-ur)—the measurement of an engine's power, abbreviated as hp

hull (HUL)—the main body of a tank or similar armored vehicle, such as the Bradley

infrared (in-fruh-RED)—able to find objects by picking up traces of heat

mission (MIH-shuhn)—a task given to a person or group

suspension (suh-SPEN-shun)—the tilting arms, springs, dampers, and other parts that smooth out road bumps so a vehicle's ride is more comfortable

track (TRAK)—on a tank or tracked vehicle, the links that form an endless loop, like a conveyor belt or "rolling road"

transmission (tranz-MISH-uhn)—gears and other parts that transfer the power from the engine to the wheels

READ MORE

Baker, David. *M2A2 Bradley Fighting Vehicle.* Fighting Forces on Land. Vero Beach, Fla.: Rourke, 2007.

Gibbs, Lynne. *Tanks.* Mega Books. North Mankato, Minn.: Chrysalis Education, 2003.

Green, Michael, and Gladys Green. *Infantry Fighting Vehicles: The M2A2 Bradleys.* War Machines. Mankato, Minn.: Capstone Press, 2004.

INTERNET SITES

FactHound offers a safe, fun way to find Internet sites related to this book. All of the sites on FactHound have been researched by our staff.

Here's how:
1. Visit *www.facthound.com*
2. Choose your grade level.
3. Type in this book ID **1429600926** for age-appropriate sites. You may also browse subjects by clicking on letters, or by clicking on pictures and words.
4. Click on the **Fetch It** button.

FactHound will fetch the best sites for you!

INDEX